Madison Valley
Places of Interest

ISABELLE GRAY

Contents

Madison Valley Boundaries

For the purposes of this book, I used the boundaries of Madison Valley as defined by the Greater Madison Valley Community Council "The area served by the Greater Madison Valley Community Council is bounded to the north by East Helen Street to Lake Washington Blvd E, to the west by 23rd Avenue East to E Denny Way, to the east by Lake Washington Boulevard to 36th Ave E then 36th Ave E south to E Denny Way, and to the south by East Denny Way."

© OpenStreetMap contributors

Explanation of Places Selected

I selected locations in and near Madison Valley that are of historic, cultural, and environmental significance. For-profit businesses have not been included. This book is meant to give an overview of and serve as an introduction to these places rather than act as a detailed deep-dive, since each place mentioned could warrant a book of its own.

Note: I chose not to include photographs of the William Grose and John Hamilton houses to respect the privacy of the current residents.

East Madison

Bailey-Boushay House

2720 East Madison Street
Seattle, WA 98112

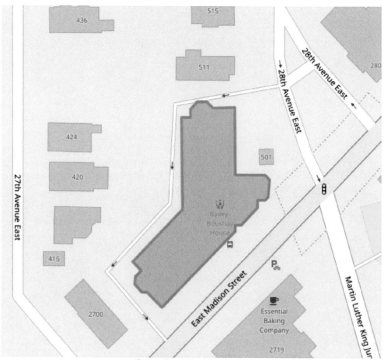

© OpenStreetMap contributors

Bailey-Boushay House offers residential care and chronic care management for people living with HIV/AIDS and other chronic illnesses. The center was

Photo: Isabelle Gray

originally founded to provide care for people living with AIDS and has expanded to provide care for other chronic afflictions, including Lou Gehrig's disease, also known as ALS.

In the late 1980s, when AIDS was still considered fatal, the number of AIDS cases was increasing in King County. Hospitals, individuals, insurance companies, and government departments were struggling to figure out how to handle the hospital costs of $600 to $800 per day per person. Seattle resident Betsy Lieberman witnessed firsthand the challenges that those diagnosed with HIV and AIDS encountered after a close friend found out that he was HIV-positive. Building on her experience as clinic coordinator at the Pike Place Market Community Clinic, she began to study the long-term care and housing needs of people with AIDS. With the help of a Robert Wood Johnson Foundation grant, the seed for Bailey-Boushay House was planted. Bailey-Boushay was named for Frank Boushay, who died of AIDS in 1989, and his partner, Thatcher Bailey. It was built by AIDS Housing of Washington (today known as Building Changes) and opened on June 24, 1992.

It was the country's first skilled nursing facility planned specifically to address the needs of people living with AIDS. On World AIDS Day, December 1, 2007, ownership of Bailey-Boushay was transferred to the Virginia Mason Health System.

Today, the center's Residential Care and Chronic Care Management programs meet the emotional, mental, physical, and medical needs of clients and residents. In 2017, Bailey-Boushay requested $500,000 from the City to open a shelter for some of their HIV-positive clients who are homeless. If funding is received, the shelter will open by January 2018.

Bailey-Boushay's first newsletter. October 1992. Source:http://www.baileybo ushay.org/documents/Hom efront/1992/Oct_1992.pdf

Photo: Isabelle Gray

Madison Park Apartments

2921 East Madison Street
Seattle, WA 98112

© OpenStreetMap contributors

This seemingly insignificant apartment building is over a century old and closely resembles its original appearance. The Madison Park Apartments were built in 1914 at the western end of the Madison Street Trestle, before the trestle was replaced with fill. (For more information on that project, see the later Trestle entry.)

Today the building houses businesses on the ground floor and residential units on the second floor. The building as it looked in 1934 is on the right of the photo below.

Photo: Isabelle Gray

Photo: East Madison Street slab job, March 6, 1934. Courtesy of the Seattle Municipal Archive, 8624.

Trestle

East Madison Street between Lake Washington Boulevard East and 29th Avenue East

© OpenStreetMap contributors

Photo: Madison street cable car, ca. 1908. courtesy of Seattle Historical Photograph Collection.

East Madison Street, east of 29th, covers what was once a trestle built for the Madison Street Cable Railway Company. In the 1860s, Judge John J. McGilvra and his wife, Elizabeth, purchased 420 acres for $5 per acre on Lake Washington, in what is now known as Madison Park. At the time, this acreage was secluded and far from the bustling activity of downtown. To make access easier, McGilvra had a road built, Madison Street, to connect his property to downtown.

At the east end of Madison Street, McGilvra created the 24-acre Madison Park, which became a popular leisure spot. As a result of Madison Park's growing popularity, McGilvra cofounded the Madison Street Cable Railway Company. The company began construction of the Madison Street Cable Car line in 1889 and completed the final extension to Madison Park in 1891.

HOW LONG, HOW LONG, ASK PATRONS OF MADISON LINE

Image: *The Seattle Star*, November 29, 1909. From *Chronicling America: Historic American Newspapers*, an online service of the Library of Congress.

Construction involved widening the street and building a large trestle bridge over the heart of Madison Valley. Trolley cars ran every two minutes, with passengers paying five cents to travel the 3.6-mile route, over the valley and a salmon stream, to Madison Park. The cable railway company also carried cargo between Lake Washington and Elliott Bay. These freight-only cars were identified with a "Lake Washington Package Freight and Express" label.

In 1900, the Madison Street Cable Car line was acquired by Seattle Electric Company. During the subsequent decade, service on the rail line was reduced because of financial troubles and aging infrastructure. When the rail line was laid, the focus had been on building a quick and inexpensive way to reach distant locations rather than on constructing durable, quality infrastructure. The trestle was eventually replaced with fill and made into a road. City of Seattle Ordinance 43542 was passed in May 1922 authorizing the Board of Public Works to fill East Madison Street between Washington Boulevard and 29th Avenue North. Another ordinance (44544) was passed just under a year later authorizing the establishment of curb grades along the same stretch of East Madison Street.

Photo: East Madison Street, March 30, 1939. Courtesy of the Seattle Municipal Archive, 38860.

Flooding

Drainage Park
(Madison Valley Stormwater Project, Phase 1)

30th Avenue East between East John Street and East Denny Way

© OpenStreetMap contributors

Madison Valley has a long history of flooding. As a result, in 1980, Seattle Public Utilities installed a 400,000-gallon stormwater detention pipe underneath 30th

Photo: Isabelle Gray

Avenue East. The system underwent improvement in the late 1990s. Following a severe storm in August 2004, which caused sewer backups and allowed stormwater to enter homes, the City purchased five parcels in the 100 block of 30th Avenue East. That land was used to create a temporary 1-million-gallon stormwater storage space. Just two years later, in December of 2006, the region experienced what came to be known as the Hanukkah Eve storm, with heavy rain and hurricane-force winds. This storm produced enough rain to cause the interim storage area to fill and overflow, with many nearby houses also flooding.

Photo: Isabelle Gray

In the wake of the Hanukkah Eve storm, the City looked into improving and enlarging stormwater retention facilities in the neighborhood. The selected solution involved two phases with a combined budget of $32 million. Phase 1 expanded the existing above-ground storage on 30th Avenue East to hold roughly 1.9 million gallons of stormwater. Phase 2 included construction of a sizable storage tank and the laying of approximately seven blocks of underground piping to join the two storage facilities. Phase 1 design began in June 2008 after the City Council and Mayor approved the project, and construction started a year later, in June 2009.

Photos: Courtesy of the Seattle Municipal Archives, 166498 & 166509.

Computer and physical models were used to establish the required storage. The block, which looks like a grassy park with steps and a winding path, is actually a large storm drain. During heavy rain it becomes a retention pond to prevent flooding. While the primary purpose of the area is to decrease the likelihood of stormwater flooding and sewer backups, the block was also created as an open space for the neighborhood.

For more information, see Storage Facility (Madison Valley Stormwater Project, Phase 2).

Photo: Isabelle Gray

Storage Facility (Madison Valley Stormwater Project, Phase 2)

Between East Madison Street and 29th Avenue East, southwest of Washington Park Playfield

© OpenStreetMap contributors

This site is Phase 2 of the Madison Valley Stormwater Project. Design of Phase 2 began in January 2009, and construction of the large storage tank started in December 2010.

Photo: Isabelle Gray

The facility became operational in November 2011. Seven blocks' worth of underground pipe connect the Phase 1 retention pond, located at 30th Avenue East between East John Street and East Denny Way, to this large tank, which can hold up to 1.3 million gallons of stormwater.

While the tank's primary purpose is the retention of stormwater, care was taken to make it and its surroundings attractive and pedestrian-friendly. There are entrances to the park-like site with connected pathways on East Madison and 29th Avenue East. Another path leads to the playfield below. The tank's façade

Councilmember Jean Godden attends ribbon cutting in Madison Valley. May 21, 2013. Photo: Courtesy of the Seattle Municipal Archive, 179827.

features synthetic and natural stone with angled stonework that creates a channel for water from the top of the tank to a rain garden below. Small cavity-nest bird sites blend into the stone to create a home for local birds. The tank is topped by a pedestrian overlook and surrounded by a reforested park. Native plants and pedestrian paths reflect elements from the nearby Arboretum.

For more information, see Drainage Park (Madison Valley Stormwater Project, Phase 1).

Photo: Isabelle Gray

Kate Fleming Memorial

East Madison Street, several yards west of the bus stop near Lake
Washington Boulevard East

© OpenStreetMap contributors

Born in 1965 in Arlington, Virginia, Kathryn Ann "Kate" Fleming was a producer, singer, and award-winning narrator. Kate graduated from the College of William & Mary with a B.A., and after a short period as an actress, she became a narrator of audiobooks under the name Anna Fields. She recorded more than 200 audiobooks and was also the owner and executive producer of Cedar House Audio, a Seattle-based production company specializing in spoken word. Kate lived on 30th Avenue East near the P-Patch with her partner, Charlene Strong.

Photo: Isabelle Gray

During the Hanukkah Eve storm of 2006, Kate died when storm drains on East Madison clogged, resulting in a flash flood that trapped Kate in her basement recording studio. After Kate's death, the City of Seattle authorized a report to ascertain the cause of flash flooding in Madison Valley. The City also built an extensive stormwater facility, part of which is located next to the Arboretum playfield and can be seen from Kate's memorial. The words inscribed on

the memorial, "Be a light. Be a flame. Be a beacon," were spoken by Kate before going on stage anytime she was to perform.

Photo: Isabelle Gray

24

Greenspaces

Harrison Ridge Greenbelt

138 32nd Avenue East
Seattle, WA 98112

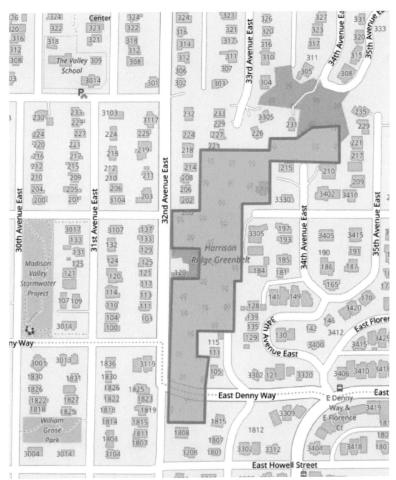

© OpenStreetMap contributors

The Harrison Ridge Greenbelt, as it exists today, is the result of community activism, several lawsuits, and government intervention. At just over six acres, the greenbelt is home to a wide array of trees, bushes, and birds.

When it came into the community's hands in the 1990s, volunteers organized work parties and tree plantings and undertook a paid work project for teens.

Photo: Isabelle Gray

Despite the greenbelt having been included in the City's greenbelt plan in 1977, in 1978 Glenn Reece purchased property on the site. A decade later he sold half to Michael and Tova Burrows. Reece and the Burrowses turned down offers from the City to purchase the land because they planned on building homes there. In 1989 King County voters approved a $117.6 million bond for open spaces, with $23.5 million set aside for acquiring greenbelt properties in Seattle. At the time, less than one-fourth of the land in the greenbelt was privately owned. The City was able to successfully negotiate with most of the owners and used some of the open space funds to buy their lots. Reece and the Burrowses were the holdouts. Following failed attempts by the City to purchase the Burrowses' and

Reece's land, the City Council passed an ordinance condemning the property in April of 1992, and it was signed by Mayor Norm Rice the following month.

Photo: Isabelle Gray

27

After the City had acquired the entire greenbelt, Blair Constantine was hired to prepare the landscape design using topographic maps. The Greater Madison Valley Community Council received a $13,000 matching grant to do the actual work. The tools loaned and volunteer hours pledged during the first year equaled the grant amount.

Photo: Charles McDade and Jerry Sussman volunteer in restoring Harrison Ridge Greenbelt. "Open Space: Central Seattle, East of I-5." Seattle Green, Summer 1998, 12.

Volunteers worked first to renew the site by removing invasive ivy and planting native species. The original forest had been cut down much earlier, so the volunteers also planted young trees in an attempt to recreate the original landscape.

An illustrated booklet called "City Woods" was created to educate people about the neighborhood's environmental

history. Students from nearby Bush School continue to help care for the greenbelt as part of an urban forestry class.

Photo: Isabelle Gray

Japanese Garden

1075 Lake Washington Boulevard East
Seattle, WA 98112

© OpenStreetMap contributors

Photos: Isabelle Gray

Located toward the south end of the Washington Park Arboretum, the Japanese Garden is among the most renowned Japanese gardens found outside of Japan. The center of the 3.5-acre garden features a semiformal space with a lake, wooden bridge, and stone peninsula. This area connects the more formal stroll-through garden to the north and the informal woodland to the south.

The garden's origins can be traced back to 1909, when Seattle hosted the Alaska-Yukon-Pacific Exposition. The exposition featured a Japanese pavilion and garden that sparked local interest and enthusiasm. In 1937, soon after the Olmsted firm designed the Arboretum, administrators decided that the Arboretum should include a Japanese garden. As the international situation deteriorated, however, they

Image: *The Seattle Star*, June 01, 1909. From *Chronicling America: Historic American Newspapers*, an online service of the Library of Congress.

agreed that the creation of that garden should be postponed until the racial/political climate was more stable. In 1957, funds were raised by the Arboretum Foundation for a Japanese garden, and Tatsuo Moriwaki of Tokyo Metro Parks was selected to oversee the process. Tatsuo chose master designers Juki Iida and Kiyoshi Inoshita to design the garden. With the design finalized in 1959, construction of the Japanese Garden was supposed to take three years, but was completed in just four months. It opened to the public in 1960.

Photos: Courtesy of the Seattle Municipal Archive, 178030 & 178034.

Once completed, the Japanese Garden became the Pacific Coast's first postwar public construction of a Japanese-style garden. As such, it has influenced the design of subsequent Japanese gardens in the region. Today, the Arboretum Foundation, a 501(c)(3) nonprofit organization, oversees events, fundraising, marketing, and recruitment of volunteers, while Seattle Parks and Recreation manages the ticket booth and plant collection. Visitors can experience tea demonstrations and presentations on certain days.

Photos: Courtesy of the Seattle Municipal Archive, 178040 & 180099.

Julia Lee's Park

2701 East Harrison Street
Seattle, WA 98112

© OpenStreetMap contributors

Julia Lee's Park was established on the southwest corner of East Harrison and Martin Luther King Jr. Way in 1993 as a memorial to native Seattleite Julia Lee Roderick Knudsen, who died in 1990. Julia was born in 1925 and lived in nearby Washington Park for a large part of her adult life. The park was built on private property by Julia's husband, C. Calvert Knudsen, as a physical representation of the love the two shared.

Photo: Isabelle Gray

The small European-style oasis was designed by local architect Glen Takagi and landscape designer Ann Smith Hunter. It contains several wooden benches situated among deciduous trees that provide shade in Seattle's increasingly hot summers. Hunter chose numerous trees and shrubs that were already mature so that the park would appear as if it had been around for a long time, and she selected low-maintenance varieties.

Photo: Isabelle Gray

For years Mr. Knudsen had an office across the street and delighted in watching members of the community enjoy the park, which was and still remains open to the public. In 2016, Julia Lee's Park was donated to the City of Seattle by the Knudsen family.

Photos: Isabelle Gray

Mercer-Madison Woods

3001 East Madison Street
Seattle, WA 98112

© OpenStreetMap contributors

The City's park website describes Mercer-Madison Woods as "a small community green space with deciduous trees and ground cover"(http://www.seattle.gov/parks/find/parks?searchType=Name&filterTerm=x64032). Easy to dismiss as a random group of trees, the one-third-acre copse is located on a hillside that was created in the early 20th century when fill material was used to grade East Madison Street. The site, which is owned by the City of Seattle, sits above and behind the Mad-P P-Patch and is home to several plant species that are characteristic of the Pacific Northwest. For nearly a century the location was ignored because the steep slope meant it could not be built upon. Due to this lack of interest, several different plant species were left to flourish, including red alder, bigleaf maple, Indian plum, and non-native English laurel, and English ivy. Unfortunately, the easy-to-miss location and lack of visibility made Mercer-Madison appealing for drug sales and consumption, and the discarding of refuse.

Community efforts to clean up the site were eventually successful. The owner of the land in the late 1980s and early

Photo: A community potluck celebrates the purchase of 3001 East Madison. Cirelli, Nick. "Open Space: Central Seattle, East of I-5." Seattle Green, Summer 1998, 12.

1990s, Robert Regan, had planned to build a 30-unit apartment building six stories high and 130 feet wide on its south side. Due to the proposed structure's size, it faced resistance from many nearby residents and the Greater Madison Valley Community Council. The Council suggested that a smaller building would be a better fit or that the City should purchase the lot and leave it unbuilt. The site had been listed as a desirable location by the Parks Department's Open Space Program, given that its trees formed a greenway link with the Arboretum, an extensively wooded Lake Washington Boulevard East, and the Harrison Ridge Greenbelt; in 1995 it was purchased by the City of Seattle Parks under the Conservation Futures Tax Bond program.

In 2001, some of the invasive species were removed. While several "trails" weave through the site, it does not contain any formal entrances. This lack of obvious entry points, combined with the steep pitch, means that any potential recreational use is limited. The site does, however, serve as a habitat for birds and small animals and contributes to the City's canopy layer. Several of the bigleaf maples previously mentioned are mature. The root structure of these large trees and of the beaked hazelnut help stabilize the hillside and reduce erosion.

Photos: Isabelle Gray

Notable African-American Residents

William Grose Park

1814 30th Avenue
Seattle, WA 98122

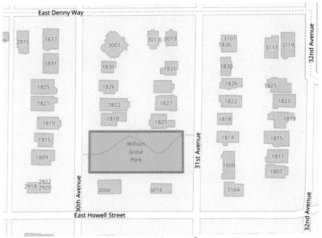

© OpenStreetMap contributors

William Grose was born in Washington D.C. in 1834. He joined the United States Navy at the age of 15 and traveled as far as Japan and the Arctic. After leaving the

Photo: Isabelle Gray

Navy, Grose worked as a gold miner in California. When racist attitudes forced him to leave, he mined in Canada. During his time as a steward on the mail-carrying boat *The Constitution*, Grose met Isaac Stevens, who was the governor of Washington. Stevens was impressed by Grose, who had found and kept safe a watch owned by the governor, and recommended that he move to Washington, at that time still a territory of the United States. Following Stevens' advice, Grose moved to Seattle in 1860, becoming the city's second African-American resident.

Image: *The Seattle Post-Intelligencer*, July 28, 1898. From *Chronicling America: Historic American Newspapers*, an online service of the Library of Congress.

He opened a restaurant called "Our House" in 1876, and in 1883 his business holdings expanded to include a downtown hotel. In 1882 Grose purchased 12 acres of land from Henry Yesler in what is now known as the Central District. At the time, the area was heavily wooded and far from the heart of activity along the waterfront. Grose lived on and farmed that land until his death on July 26, 1898.

WILLIAM GROSE IS DEAD.

PIONEER COLORED RESIDENT AND LARGEST MAN IN THE STATE.

He Was Six Feet Two Inches In Height and Weighed 420 Pounds Casket Cannot Be Taken Into the House—A Friend of Gov. Stevens.

William Grose, colored, died early yesterday morning at the family residence...

Image: *The Seattle Post-Intelligencer*, July 27, 1898. From *Chronicling America: Historic American Newspapers*, an online service of the Library of Congress.

In addition to being a successful business owner, William Grose helped to establish an African-American community in Seattle by developing and selling parts of his land to African-American families. Grose also helped to finance *The Elevator*, an African-American newspaper on the West Coast, and he acted as an important connection in the Underground Railroad, using his network to shepherd slaves to British Columbia. Shortly before he died, Grose's holdings were estimated to be worth a quarter of a million dollars. So many mourners attended his funeral that the 16 carriages provided were not sufficient to transport them all to his burial place in Lake View Cemetery.

A mini-park between East Denny Way and East Howell covering four residential lots and called 30th Avenue East Park was created under the administration of Walter Hundley, director of the Seattle Model City Program from 1968 until 1974. Less than a decade after its creation, a group of neighborhood residents known as Madison Valley Concerned Citizens petitioned the City to rename the park after William Grose, "a name that honors and acknowledges the important role that black people played in settling and developing Seattle's communities, especially the Madison Valley" (*Valley View*, January 2000).

41

As a result of this renaming push, Seattle's superintendent of Parks and Recreation designated the 30th Avenue mini-park as William Grose Park in 1983.

Photo: Isabelle Gray

Photo: Isabelle Gray

William Grose House

1733 24th Avenue
Seattle, WA 98122

© OpenStreetMap contributors

There is some disagreement about whether William Grose's house is located at 1733 or 1735 24th Avenue. According to the City of Seattle, the house located at 1733 was Grose's home from around 1890 until his death in 1898. Although the two-story dwelling has undergone some alteration (the Victorian porch was removed and replaced with a Tudoresque stoop), it has kept its basic form. The 1904–1905 Sanborn Map indicates that the house was originally built on a large parcel and faced toward the north, even though the north-facing direction had no clear correlation to the streets as they existed at the time. Sometime before 1910, the structure was moved to face 24th Avenue and the east. It shares a staircase with the house at 1735, which was also a Grose family house.

Photo: *Black Past Online Encyclopedia*, public domain.

For more information on William Grose, see William Grose Park.

Homer Harris Park

2401 East Howell Street
Seattle, WA 98122

© OpenStreetMap contributors

This half-acre park is named for Dr. Homer Eugene Harris Jr., an admired and respected Seattle athlete and doctor. Dr. Harris was born March 4, 1916, in Seattle, to Mattie Vineyard Harris, a Seattle native, and Homer Eugene Harris Sr., who was from Gastonia, North Carolina, and worked as a postal clerk. Homer grew up less than a mile from the park that would one day bear his name, in the Harris family home at 2507 Helen Street near the Washington Park Arboretum. Harris's maternal aunt also lived nearby, next to the Japanese Garden.

As a child Harris attended Stevens Elementary School, and in 1933, while a student at Garfield High School, he became the first African-American football team captain. When it came time for college, he avoided the University of Washington because of racist attitudes and the fact that, as an African-American, he would not have been allowed to live on campus. He instead, with the help of a football scholarship, attended the University of Iowa, where he was voted Most Valuable Player in 1937. That same year he became the first African-American captain of a Big Ten team and the first African-American captain of any sport in the

Photo: Isabelle Gray

state of Iowa. Harris wanted to play professional football after graduation; however, the National Football League had banned African-American players.

With his professional football hopes dashed, Harris accepted a position coaching football at A&T College in Greensboro, North Carolina. Mattie Harris hoped that her only son would become a physician, so with her prodding, Homer enrolled in Meharry Medical College in Nashville, Tennessee. After completing his medical degree, Dr. Harris joined the Army.

Photo: Public domain

Following World War II, he interned in Kansas City, Missouri, and then trained in dermatology with Dr. T. K. Lawless at the University of Illinois in Chicago. He selected dermatology as his specialization because as a dermatologist he would not need to rely on a hospital or referrals from other physicians.

Harris moved back to Seattle in 1955 and opened his dermatology practice in the Medical Dental Building downtown. Opening an office in this location turned out to be a challenge due to his color. He was initially told by the building manager that no space was available. Dr. Harris doubted the truthfulness of this statement and related his experience to Stimson Bullitt, an influential Seattleite. Soon after that phone call with Bullitt, the building manager visited Dr. Harris's home to offer him office space. Over the years, Dr. Harris became a well-known and respected dermatologist in Seattle. It was said that his practice was the largest west of the Rocky Mountains. He retired in 2000 after 43 years of practicing medicine. In November 2002, the City announced that an anonymous benefactor had donated $1.3 million to build a park in honor of the doctor. At the time, the donation was the largest single private donation for a park in Seattle's history. November 13, 2002, was declared Dr. Homer

Harris Day by the state of Washington.

This park is on land that was once owned by William Grose (see William Grose Park), who purchased the parcel from Henry Yesler for $1,000 in gold in 1882. The park's location offers views of the Cascade Mountains and Lake Washington. Even after all that he had achieved, Dr. Harris remained humble; in response to the

Photo: Courtesy of the Seattle Municipal Archive, 133537.

anonymous donation he said, "I'm very imperfect, and I've struggled just like everybody else" (http://www.aaregistry.org/historic_events/view/homer-harris-one-seattles-finest). Harris was honored in 1989 by the Black Heritage Society of Washington State as a black pioneer in dermatology, and in 2002 he was inducted into the University of Iowa Hall of Fame for his athletic abilities and the barriers he had overcome. The induction, which he attended with his grandson, was the first time Dr. Harris had visited the university since

Photos: Courtesy of the Seattle Municipal Archive, 133516, & 133550.

graduation. In 2003, the African American Sports Hall of Fame's Pacific Northwest chapter followed suit and inducted Harris.

Homer Harris Park opened to the public on May 14, 2005. Dr. Harris passed away in his Queen Anne home from Alzheimer's disease on March 17, 2007, at 90 years of age. He was preceded in death by his wife of 56 years, Dorothy, who died in 2005.

Photos: Isabelle Gray

John H. "Doc" Hamilton House

417 29th Avenue East
Seattle, WA 98112

© OpenStreetMap contributors

Another once-famous Madison Valley resident, Mississippi-raised John Henry "Doc" Hamilton, was an African-American owner/manager of several of Seattle's speakeasies during Prohibition. Doc was a veteran of the renowned 92nd (Buffalo) Division in World War I. His establishments were patronized by a spectrum of local citizens, including members of Seattle's European-American privileged families. His businesses had many names, including the famous Barbecue Pit, also known as the 908 Club, at 908 12th Avenue.

In 1923, Doc showed his civic spirit by sponsoring the Queen City All-Stars baseball team. Seattleites who knew him well described his sense of humor, engaging manner, and business acumen. Apparently he had detractors as well: following a scuffle in one of his bars, several of Doc's "good friends" turned him in to authorities for selling alcohol. He served a brief term in prison and later died alone in Chinatown's Mar Hotel on September 8, 1942.

Doc's European-style home at 417 29th Avenue East still stands today.

Hamilton's World War I Draft Registration Card: United States World War I Draft Registration Cards, 1917-1918, database with images, FamilySearch (https://familysearch.org/ark:/61903/1:1:QJDG-4RHH : 11 June 2014), John Henry Hamilton, 1917-1918; citing Seattle City no 10, Washington, United States, NARA microfilm publication M1509 (Washington D.C.: National Archives and Records Administration, n.d.); FHL microfilm 1,991,928.

Prentis I. Frazier Park

401 24th Avenue East
Seattle, WA 98112

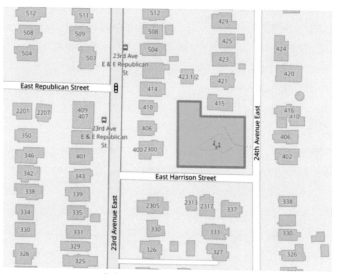

© OpenStreetMap contributors

Prentis Frazier was born in 1880 in Jasper County, Texas. His parents, Armstead and Martha Frazier, were both former slaves, and Prentis had little formal schooling. Prentis left home at a young age, first going to Beaumont and later to Dallas, Texas. After the failure of various entrepreneurial ventures, including banking and running a boarding house, he and his wife, Clara, moved north and

Photo: Isabelle Gray

ultimately established themselves in Seattle. Frazier had business dealings in bail bonds, insurance, and real estate.

With a focus on assisting African-American businesses, he helped establish Blackwell and Johnson Undertakers in 1920, and in 1925 he partnered with Clarence Anderson to open Anzier Movie Theater. Several years later, Frazier and William Wilson founded and began publishing an African-American-focused newspaper called *Seattle Enterprise*. The paper, later renamed *Northwest Enterprise*, was published until the 1950s. Frazier resided in the Central Area the entire time he lived in Seattle. He made his home at 410 23rd Avenue East during the last decade of his life. In 1970, the gully behind his house was turned into the one-third-acre Harrison Street Mini Park, which in 1983 the Seattle Parks and Recreation Department renamed Prentis I. Frazier Park.

P. FRAZIER

REAL ESTATE, INSURANCE,
Loans and Collections

316 PACIFIC BLOCK   SEATTLE, WASH.
Phone Main 4554

Image: *Cayton's weekly*. (Seattle, Wash.), May 22 1920. From *Chronicling America: Historic American Newspapers,* an online service of the Library of Congress.

FRAZIER SOLD THE DIRT

During the year 1919 P. Frazier, the real estate dealer, made many individual realty sales. A partial list of which is herewith shown:

M. M. Rogers	$2,450
Wm. Barnes	5,000
B. Williams	4,500
P. M. Foster	3,500
A. J. Bufford	2,500
Pearl White	4,500
C. R. Anderson	15,200
Cena Donegan	4,500
Frazier & Anderson	19,850
R. Smith	15,000
W. A. Hylyard	3,000
R. Wattan	4,200
Mrs. Lyda Harris	2,500
Mrs. P. M. Major	4,000
W. Hallum	2,400
E. Richardson	3,650
M. Tutor	15,000
J. N. Drake	1,500
Willis Greene	2,500
Geo. Bright	3,000

Joseph Due	500
Sojourner Truth Club	7,500
Mable Mann	14,500
Maud Everett	7,000
E. Miller	2,000
N. Slaughter	2,000
Mrs. H. V. Ray	2,750
Mr. A. Adam	3,000
Thos. Wilson	2,500
Mrs. Wm. Jackson	2,300
J. W. Phillip	3,000
Jas. S. McBae	1,500
Mrs. J. B. White	2,400
G. H. Blackwell	1,900
Richard Smith	2,500
Mrs. Barnes	2,200
W. E. Vrooman	3,375
Mrs. Lulu Jackson	10,000
M. W. Coleman	38,500
M. Brooks	3,150
W. M. Biggs	6,500
Charles Newton	3,150
Mrs. A. B. Henriquez	3,250
William Nelson	1,000
Mae Harris	3,400
Mary Jones	3,500

In addition to the above sales I have written about $200,000 worth of fire insurance.

P. FRAZIER,
316 Pacific Block
Telephone Mani 4554.

Image: *Cayton's weekly*. (Seattle, Wash.), December 27 1919. From *Chronicling America: Historic American Newspapers,* an online service of the Library of Congress.

In 2016, the Seattle Park District contributed $400,000 for renovation of the park, including replacement of the playground equipment. Community input was solicited and incorporated into the renovation plans. As of summer 2017, construction is slated to begin in fall 2017.

Photos: Isabelle Gray

Olmsted Influence

Washington Park Arboretum

2300 Arboretum Drive East

Seattle, WA 98112

© OpenStreetMap contributors

The Washington Park Arboretum has one of the most diverse plant collections in North America. In 1900, the City of Seattle received a donation of a 62-acre tract from the Puget Mill Company. This tract, a former streambed, would form the first version of the Arboretum.

Photos: Isabelle Gray

In 1934, after the City had added to the initial 62 acres through several acquisitions and purchases, Ordinance #65130 permitted the establishment and maintenance of a botanical garden and arboretum in Washington Park. In 1935, The Board of Park Commissioners entered into a contract with the renowned Olmsted firm to design the park. With the initial design finalized in March of 1936, work on the garden was completed in 1940.

Photos: Seattle Arboretum, November 1934. Courtesy of the Seattle Municipal Archive, 77272 & 77273.

Originally called University of Washington Arboretum, the name was officially changed in 1974 to Washington Park Arboretum.

That same year, a new agreement between the University and the City was signed, updating how the 1934 agreement would be executed. It specified that the Arboretum would be mainly a space for public use and that no new buildings were to be constructed unless they replaced existing structures or were meant to serve the public. The first version of the Washington Park Arboretum featured a formal rose garden where there is now a soccer field. Today's Azalea Way was formerly used as an unofficial track for racing horses.

Photo: Washington Park. Azalia Way Speed Way. Arboretum. 1908. Courtesy of the Seattle Municipal Archive, 30553.

Eventually, the City and the University of Washington made a deal to expand the Arboretum to its current 230 acres of woodlands, wetlands, gardens, and walking trails. Its plant collections include hollies, oaks, camellias, Japanese maples, and conifers. Currently, the Arboretum's ownership and management are a collaboration between the City of Seattle and the University of Washington (UW). The City owns the land and handles maintenance of park-like functions, including the trails, benches, and garbage. The UW owns the plant collections and trees, and the UW's Botanic Gardens unit maintains the Arboretum's plants, trees, and gardens. In addition, the Arboretum and Botanical Garden Committee (ABGC), representing a range of constituents, "advises the University of Washington, City of Seattle and The Arboretum Foundation on the management and stewardship of the Washington Park Arboretum for the benefit of current and future generations" (http://depts.washington.edu/wpa/abgc/).

Photo: Barn for the Arboretum service area built by the WPA in 1936. Courtesy of the Seattle Municipal Archive, 30560.

After the ABGC was formed in 1936 as stipulated by the 1934 agreement between the University and the City, one of its first tasks was to create the Arboretum Foundation to raise funds for the Arboretum's creation and maintenance. The Foundation still plays a significant part in funding Arboretum programs.

In 2001, the University, the Arboretum Foundation, and Seattle Parks and Recreation completed a new master plan for the Arboretum. It underscored the need for more user-friendliness via better accessibility and increased public education. One large-scale development that resulted from this master plan is the Washington Park Arboretum Loop Trail. This multi-use trail for

Photo: Isabelle Gray

pedestrians and bicyclists is meant to enrich the visitor experience. The City Council approved $7.8 million in 2013 for the trail, and construction began in spring of 2016. As of this book's writing, the first section of the trail, at the south end of the Arboretum, had been opened.

Photo: Isabelle Gray

Lake Washington Boulevard East

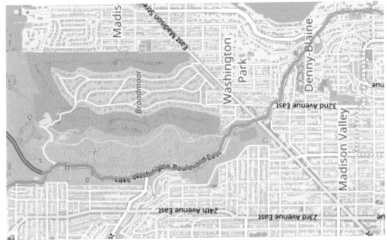

© OpenStreetMap contributors

This tree-lined road is 9.2 miles (14.8 km) in length and serves as the eastern boundary of Madison Valley. It extends from the Montlake neighborhood in the north where it is called East Lake Washington Boulevard to Seward Park in the south where it is named Lake Washington Boulevard. Designed by John Charles Olmsted (JCO) of the same Olmsted firm that planned the Washington Park Arboretum, Lake Washington Boulevard was

conceived as a respite from city life. JCO envisaged the road as a scenic "pleasure drive" that would integrate into and take advantage of Seattle's striking landscape and changing topography.

John Charles Olmsted. Photo: Seattle Municipal Archives, Courtesy of the National Park Service, Frederick Law Olmsted National Historic Site. 172640.

Following the Klondike Gold Rush in 1897, Seattle experienced tremendous growth and city leaders focused on implementing a park system influenced by the City Beautiful movement. The plan had been temporarily shelved several years earlier due to a recession. Seattle park commissioners invited Olmsted Brothers Landscape Architects to visit Seattle and in 1903, following a trip to Portland to advise the City on plans for the 1905 Lewis & Clark Exposition, JCO then traveled north to Seattle to draw up a proposal for a park system. During his month-long visit in the spring of 1903, Olmsted met with park commissioners and journeyed throughout Seattle via boat, foot, and streetcar. After returning home to Brookline, Massachusetts in June, JCO submitted his final proposal to Seattle park commissioners in July of the same year. Olmsted's plans were approved by the commissioners in autumn and adopted by the City Council on November 16, 1903.

JCO's plan contained suggestions for development of existing parks as well as land acquisition for new parks. The larger parks were to be connected by boulevards and Lake Washington Boulevard was a crucial component of this system. While Olmsted came up with the vision for Seattle's boulevard scheme, Seattle's Board of Park Commissioners and Engineering Department played integral roles in implementing JCO's ideas. Under the supervision of Park Superintendent John W. Thompson and Chief Engineer Reginald H. Thomson, city employees built the road in segments beginning, in 1904, with a section in Washington Park. As part of preparations for the Alaska-Yukon-Pacific Exposition, city leaders pressed for the construction of roads and streetcar lines to transport visitors to the Exposition location at the University of Washington campus. The Board of Park Commissioners stated in their 1909 annual report "Special efforts were made and heavy expenditures were required in carrying out our plan to have our north and south chain of boulevards along or overlooking Lake Washington from

Souvenir guide of the Alaska-Yukon-Pacific Exposition. 1909. Image courtesy of Seattle Public Library Alaska-Yukon-Pacific Exposition Digital Collection.

the Mount Baker district, north to the Exposition grounds, open for traffic, so that our Eastern visitors might enjoy the beauties of our lake and mountain scenery."
(http://www.historylink.org/File/10244). More than five miles of the boulevard were constructed in time for the exposition.

The final portion of Lake Washington Boulevard was completed in 1917. During the 1930s, the boulevard underwent significant upgrades thanks to support from the Works Progress Administration (WPA), Seattle's Department of Streets and Sewers, and Board of Parks Commissioners. The improvements included retaining wall construction, and restoration of a deteriorating section of the road. Several years later, in

Motorists Are Urged to Get Behind Boulevard Movement

Immediate action should be taken to pave the Newport-Renton stretch of the Lake Washington boulevard if the beauties of that matchless thorofare are to be preserved so that Seattle and King county may boast of a lake-circling highway equal to any scenic driveway in the nation.

This is the consensus of opinion of hundreds of country good roads boosters and motorists who have pledged their support to a campaign to have the Lake Washington boulevard paved, which was inaugurated two weeks ago by the Automobile Club of Western Washington. Petitions urging the county commissioners to immediately finance the project were liberally signed and mailed to the club's Seattle headquarters by a large number of residents, while many personal assurances of support have been received from all sections of the county. However, a more concerted support on the part of all residents is necessary if the Newport to Renton stretch is to be paved by next summer. The petition accompanies

until Bellevue is reached on the eastern side of the lake.

From Bellevue to Newport, a distance of four miles, the boulevard is to be paved, the contract having already been awarded. This stretch will be ready for paving in about a year, when the new grading shall have settled sufficiently to support paving.

The last unsightly gap that still remains to mar the natural beauty of the Lake Washington boulevard is that portion of the highway extending seven miles between Newport and Renton. This is the stretch that the Automobile Club of Western Washington, at the instance of 40,000 county motorists and the public in general, is campaigning to have paved immediately. Of course,

I WANT THE LAKE WASHINGTON BOULEVARD PAVED

Seattle.........................

I am a King county citizen, anxious for the development of our natural and scenic resources, and herewith demand immediate action in paving the 11-mile stretch of the Lake Washington boulevard between Bellevue, Newport and Renton.

Signed.........................

Address.........................

Image: *The Seattle Star,* August 9 1919. From *Chronicling America: Historic American Newspapers,* an online service of the Library of Congress.

1942, the City's Engineering Department assumed responsibility for maintaining the boulevard south of the Arboretum. As funds became available, further improvements to drainage and paving were implemented during the next decade.

Throughout the years, as the city has grown, the boulevard has continued to offer views of the adjoining parks and lakeshore for those traveling its curving length via foot, bicycle, and automobile. In the 1980s, a landscape study of the boulevard was carried out resulting in design enhancement recommendations such as improved drainage and integration of bicycle travel. 2010 saw the City of Seattle finalize a vegetation management plan with guidance for maintaining the health of roadside plants. Due to its historic significance, Lake Washington Boulevard was listed on the National Register of Historic Places in May 2017.

Photo: Isabelle Gray

P-Patches

Mad-P P-Patch

3000 East Mercer Street
Seattle, WA 98112

© OpenStreetMap contributors

The Mad-P P-Patch is located at the northern end of 30th Avenue East and covers 2,500 square feet. In 2000, Sarah Trethewey, a Madison Valley resident, began attending Greater Madison Valley Community Council (MVCC) meetings, and when the council requested suggestions for what could be done in the neighborhood, Sarah suggested a P-Patch.

The P-Patch location sits at the end of a quiet residential street at the bottom of Mercer-Madison Woods. The site had long been neglected and was sometimes the location of illegal drug activity. While MVCC was supportive of establishing a P-Patch, the council left it to community members to bring

Photo: Isabelle Gray

the idea to fruition. Sarah managed the grant application and partnered with a high school volunteer who used the project as her senior-year assignment. The two of them applied for and received a matching grant on behalf of MVCC from the City of Seattle. That "Neighborhood Matching Fund Small and Simple

Grant" enabled community members to purchase the necessary equipment and materials to build the P-Patch and create the water connection. The grant was matched with volunteer hours and donations of tools, plants, and various gardening items. After a year of designing and preparing the P-Patch site, and gaining neighborhood support, the P-Patch was ready for planting in May 2001; it has been in continuous use since then. In addition to the 17 individual plots, Mad-P also has a large "giving garden" set aside for food bank donations, a community herb garden, and a raspberry patch. Donation recipients include Northwest Harvest, St. Mary's Food Bank, and Cherry Street Food Bank.

Photo: Isabelle Gray

Ida Mia Garden

East Madison Street & Lake Washington Boulevard East

© OpenStreetMap contributors

At 1,600 square feet, this hidden garden is one of the smallest in Seattle's P-Patch Community Gardening Program.

Photo: Isabelle Gray

Photo: Isabelle Gray

Created in 1994 and named after the property owners' daughter, Ida Mia Garden has seven plots and is accessed by the alley on East Madison east of Lake Washington Boulevard. While not as well maintained as the nearby Mad-P P-Patch, the Ida Mia Garden is a pleasant surprise for those who stumble upon it in the middle of surrounding apartments and businesses.

School and Community Space

Bush School

3400 East Harrison Street
Seattle, WA 98112

© OpenStreetMap contributors

In 1924, Helen Taylor Bush opened a preschool and kindergarten in her home at 133 Dorffel Drive, with an initial enrollment of

Photo: Isabelle Gray

six students. During the next few years, Helen's focus on the fine arts, nature, and the sciences resulted in the school's expansion to six grades, beyond the capacity of Helen's home. As a result of this growth, Helen rented the buildings at Harrison and Lake Washington Boulevard that had housed the former Lakeside School. In 1929, the school became a nonprofit with a board of trustees. The following year, the school both expanded and divided. The Lower School, which was coeducational through sixth grade, was given the name Parkside; the Upper School, called the Helen Bush School for Girls, covered grades seven and eight and was single-gender (due to the terms of the rental agreement). The combined school was named Helen Bush–Parkside School.

In 1941, nearly two decades after opening Bush School in her home, Helen Bush went on to influence education throughout the region by helping to organize the Pacific Northwest Association of Independent Schools, today called simply the Northwest Association of Independent Schools, or NWAIS (http://www.nwais.org/). In 1948, Helen Taylor Bush passed away, just three months after resigning from the school that still carries her name. In 1970, the Upper School began accepting boy students, making that institution, formally renamed the Bush School, the city's only independent, coeducational school serving grades K through 12. Today, the Bush School's eleven buildings sit on a nine-acre campus next to the MLK F.A.M.E. Community Center.

Photo: Isabelle Gray

MLK F.A.M.E. Community Center

3201 East Republican Street
Seattle, WA 98112

© OpenStreetMap contributors

The building that houses the Martin Luther King Jr. Family, Arts, Mentoring & Enrichment (F.A.M.E.) Community Center was built in 1913 as the Harrison School. Named after the United States' 23rd president, Benjamin Harrison, to educate the children of workers employed by industrial and shipyard trades, the school began with grades 1 through 4. In 1918, the PTA asked the school board to expand the building according to previously abandoned blueprints so that students in grades 5 and above would not have to attend other schools. In the 1920s, the school added grades 5 and 6. The school closed, except for a single grade-1 classroom, in July 1932, following the end of World War I. A decline in both the population and industrial employment had resulted in such dwindling enrollment that the per-student cost had become excessive.

In 1934, the entire school was shut down due to inadequate enrollment. Thanks to appeals by the neighborhood, the school reopened as Harrison Grade School in 1936 with two rooms for grades 1 through 3. The Harrison PTA steered community involvement and eventually led to the formation of a community council. In 1954, a community group asked the school board to widen the school's boundaries to preserve racial balance.

Harrison School P.-T. A.
Will entertain with a social at 1:15 p. m. Program by pupils of the school. All parents are urged to attend. Refreshments served.

Image: *The Seattle Star,* November 25, 1919. From *Chronicling America: Historic American Newspapers,* an online service of the Library of Congress.

In reply to the group's request, the superintendent explained that Harrison had been reopened only to avoid overcrowding at nearby schools and Harrison's facilities could not support much further expansion. Despite this explanation, four years later an addition including eight classrooms, a playcourt, a gymnasium, and a lunchroom/auditorium was built. This 1958 remodel extended the front of the building so that it now stretches the length of 32nd Avenue East between East Republican and Harrison. Following the building expansion, the school's boundaries were broadened to accommodate students residing north of Madison. In the spring of 1974, students voted to rename the school Martin Luther King Jr. Elementary School, a change that was approved by the school board. The school returned to serving grades K through 5 in 1989. In the ensuing years, MLK Jr. Elementary was Seattle School District's smallest elementary school. In spite of lawsuits and protests, the Seattle School District closed Martin Luther King Jr. Elementary School in 2006 because of the small size of the student body. (That year the school had 100 students, while the standard size of other public schools in Seattle ranged from 300 to 500.)

In 2010, the Seattle School Board voted 5 to 2 to sell the vacant building to First African Methodist Episcopal (AME) Church. First AME bid against two other groups, the

Photo: Isabelle Gray

school's immediate neighbor the Bush School, and Citizens for a Community Center at MLK (CCC@MLK). While First AME and CCC@MLK submitted similar bids of $2.4 million, it was the church's offer of "substantial support for youth education activities, in the form of free access to the gym and auditorium and reduced rent for at least five classrooms, for 40 years" (http://www.madisonparktimes.com/Content/News/Top-Stories/Article/From-conflict-to-community/26/284/28612) that made a difference. The youth education support offered was valued at roughly $1 million. The Bush School offered $5.6

million in exchange for a 99-year lease. If successful, Bush had planned to demolish the building and install an athletic field. The school district's decision to proceed with First AME's bid was controversial and resulted in accusations of fraud and an investigation by the state Auditor's Office. The district denied any artifice or conflict of interest. After ownership of the building was transferred, the new MLK F.A.M.E. Community Center focused on outreach to the community and implementing building upgrades to pass inspections. Today, First AME Church acts as the parent organization and allows the center to run independently, governed by the MLK Community Center's own board of directors. The center is a nonprofit organization dedicated to promoting social, cultural, economic, and community service for Seattle-area residents of all ages, races, cultures, and ethnicities. It also leases space to tenants supportive of Madison Valley and the surrounding communities. Revenue from the leased rooms, subsidized by grants and contributions, funds the center's programming.

Photo: Isabelle Gray

Bibliography

"3001 E Madison Park." Seattle Parks and Recreation. Accessed July 08, 2017. https://www.seattle.gov/parks/find/parks/3001-e-madison-park.

"About Bailey-Boushay House." Bailey-Boushay House. Accessed February 20, 2017. http://www.bailey-boushay.org/.

"About Us." Seattle Japanese Garden. Accessed February 20, 2017. https://www.seattlejapanesegarden.org/about-us-index.

"About Washington Park Arboretum." Arboretum Foundation. Accessed February 20, 2017. https://www.arboretumfoundation.org/about-us/about-the-arboretum/.

Angelos, Constantine. "City Vs. Owners Over Greenbelt Area— Seattle Condemnation Orders Spark Lot Holders to Vow to Fight to End." *Seattle Times*, June 9, 1992. Accessed June 29, 2017. http://community.seattletimes.nwsource.com/archive/?date=19920609&slug=1496319.

"Appreciation." *Valley View*, issue 105 (September 2002).

"Arboretum and Botanical Garden Committee (ABGC)." University of Washington Botanic Gardens. Accessed July 08, 2017. http://depts.washington.edu/wpa/abgc/.

"Area We Serve." Greater Madison Valley Community Council. Accessed July 09, 2017.

https://www.madisonvalleycommunitycouncil.org/area-we-serve-1/.

"Bailey-Boushay House." Virginia Mason Medical Center. Accessed February 20, 2017. https://www.virginiamason.org/dept.cfm?id=474.

Burns, Ian. "Central District Green Spaces Honor Local Black Leaders." *Real Change*, March 10, 2011. Accessed July 08, 2017. http://realchangenews.org/2011/03/10/central-district-green-spaces-honor-local-black-leaders.

Carriveau, Anna. "Forest Stewards Make Headway with Local Greenbelt." *Madison Park Times*, February 1, 2016. Accessed February 20, 2017. http://www.madisonparktimes.com/Content/News/Top-Stories/Article/Forest-Stewards-make-headway-with-local-greenbelt/26/284/30424.

"CD History: How Segregation Shaped the Neighborhood." *Central District News*, July 22, 2010. Accessed February 20, 2017. http://www.centraldistrictnews.com/2010/07/cd-history-how-segregation-shaped-the-neighborhood/.

"Clerk File Number: 310309; Department of Parks and Recreation's Rule No. 060-P 5.11.1, Relating to Park Classification System." Office of the City Clerk. December 1, 2009. Accessed February 20, 2017. http://clerk.ci.seattle.wa.us/~scripts/nph-brs.exe?s1=Grose&S2=&Sect4=AND&l=0&Sect1=IMAGE&Sect2=THESON&Sect3=PLURON&Sect5=LEGI2&Sect6=HITOFF&d=LEGA

&p=1&u=%2F~public%2Flegisearch.htm&r=5&f=G.

"Council Bill Number: 33100; Ordinance Number: 43542." Office of the City Clerk. Accessed April 23, 2017. http://clerk.ci.seattle.wa.us/~scripts/nph-brs.exe?s1=madison%2Bfill&S2=%28%40dtir%3E19200000%3C19300000%29%2BOR%2B%28%40DTA%3E19200000%3C19300000%29%2BOR%2B%28%40DTS%3E19200000%3C19300000%29%2BOR%2B%28%40DTSI%3E19200000%3C19300000%29%2BOR%2B%2B%28%40DTMY%3E19200000%3C19300000%29%2BOR%2B%28%40DATE%3E19200000%3C19300000%29%2BOR%2B%28%40dtf%3E19200000%3C19300000%29&Sect4=AND&l=0&Sect1=IMAGE&Sect2=THESON&Sect3=PLURON&Sect5=LEGI2&Sect6=HITOFF&d=LEGA&p=1&u=%2F~public%2Flegisearch.htm&r=7&f=G.

"Council Bill Number: 33742; Ordinance Number: 44544." Office of the City Clerk. Accessed April 23, 2017. http://clerk.ci.seattle.wa.us/~scripts/nph-brs.exe?s1=madison%2Bfill&S2=%28%40dtir%3E19200000%3C19300000%29%2BOR%2B%28%40DTA%3E19200000%3C19300000%29%2BOR%2B%28%40DTS%3E19200000%3C19300000%29%2BOR%2B%28%40DTSI%3E19200000%3C19300000%29%2BOR%2B%2B%28%40DTMY%3E19200000%3C19300000%29%2BOR%2B%28%40DATE%3E19200000%3C19300000%29%2BOR%2B%28%40dtf%3E19200000%3C19300000%29&Sect4=AND&l=0&Sect1=IMAGE&Sect2=THESON&Sect3=PLURON&Sect5=LEGI2&Sect6=HITOFF&d=LEGA&p=1&u=%2F~public%2Flegisearch.htm&r=6&f=G.

Eskenazi, David. "Wayback Machine: A Legacy of Black

Baseball." *Sportspress Northwest*. May 15, 2015. Accessed July 08, 2017. http://sportspressnw.com/2203231/2015/wayback-machine-a-legacy-of-black-baseball.

"Giving Garden List." Seattle's Giving Garden Network. Accessed July 08, 2017. http://www.sggn.org/maps/giving-garden-list/.

Glass, Shannon. "Prentis Frazier Park Play Area Renovation." Seattle Parks and Recreation. Accessed July 29, 2017. https://www.seattle.gov/parks/about-us/current-projects/prentis-frazier-park-play-area-renovation.

"Harrison Ridge Greenbelt Revisited." *Valley View*, issue 106 (October 2002).

Henry, Mary. "Frazier, Prentis (1880–1959)." HistoryLink.org. May 27, 1999. Accessed July 08, 2017. http://www.historylink.org/File/1166.

Henry, Mary. "Grose, William (1835–1898)." HistoryLink.org. November 27, 1998. Accessed March 16, 2017. http://www.historylink.org/File/393.

Henry, Mary. "Hundley, Walter R. (1929-2002)." BlackPast.org. Accessed July 20, 2017. http://www.blackpast.org/aaw/hundley-walter-r-1929-2002.

Henry, Mary T. "Harris, Dr. Homer E. Jr. (1916–2007)." HistoryLink.org. September 2, 2014. Accessed February 20, 2017. http://www.historylink.org/File/4222.

Hildreth, Casey. "The Crossroads of Seattle's Disappearing 'Blackscape': Madison Street at 23rd Avenue." University of Washington, Department of Urban Planning. http://courses.washington.edu/ordinary/Casey.Final_Paper.pdf.

"History of BBH." Bailey-Boushay House. Accessed February 20, 2017. http://www.bailey-boushay.org/history.

Hodges, Brett, John Logan, Blaine Onishi, Jennifer Van Wagoner, and Kaila Yun. "Mercer Madison Woods." Washington State University Puyallup Research and Extension Center. Winter 2004, EHUF 480. Accessed February 20, 2017. https://puyallup.wsu.edu/lcs/wp-content/uploads/sites/403/2015/03/MercerMad.pdf.

"Homer Harris, One of Seattle's Finest." African American Registry. Accessed February 20, 2017. http://www.aaregistry.org/historic_events/view/homer-harris-one-seattles-finest.

"Homer Harris Park." Seattle Parks and Recreation. Accessed February 20, 2017. https://www.seattle.gov/parks/find/parks/homer-harris-park.

"Julia Lee's Park." Seattle Parks and Recreation. Accessed February 20, 2017. http://www.seattle.gov/parks/find/parks/julia-lee%E2%80%99s-park.

"Julia Lee's Park." Year of Seattle Parks. October 5, 2016. Accessed July 08, 2017.

http://www.yearofseattleparks.com/2016/10/05/julia-lees-park/.

"Kate Fleming." Wikipedia. Accessed February 20, 2017. https://en.wikipedia.org/wiki/Kate_Fleming.

Kelleher, Susan, and Sonia Krishnan. "State Investigates Seattle District's Sale of MLK School." *Seattle Times*, June 5, 2011. Accessed July 08, 2017. http://www.seattletimes.com/seattle-news/state-investigates-seattle-districts-sale-of-mlk-school/.

Kohnert, Janelle. "Community Coming to Terms with First AME Church Moving into Old School." *Madison Park Times*, November 3, 2010. Accessed February 20, 2017. http://madisonparktimes.com/Content/News/Top-Stories/Article/Community-coming-to-terms-with-First-AME-Church-moving-into-old-school/26/284/27920.

Lacao, Alberto, Jr. "From conflict to community." *Madison Park Times*, October 04, 2012. Accessed February 20, 2017. http://www.madisonparktimes.com/Content/News/Top-Stories/Article/From-conflict-to-community/26/284/28612.

"Madison Valley 'Mad-P.'" Seattle Department of Neighborhoods. Accessed February 20, 2017. http://www.seattle.gov/neighborhoods/programs-and-services/p-patch-community-gardening/p-patch-list/madison-valley.

Mars, Shaun Michael. "Harris, Jr., Dr. Homer E. (1916–2007)." BlackPast.org. Accessed February 20, 2017. http://www.blackpast.org/aaw/harris-jr-dr-homer-e-1916-2007.

Mays, Darla. "Kathryn 'Kate' Fleming." FindAGrave.com. December 15, 2006. Accessed February 20, 2017. http://www.findagrave.com/cgi-bin/fg.cgi?page=gr&GRid=17035616.

"Mission, Philosophy & History." The Bush School. Accessed February 20, 2017. http://www.bush.edu/page/about-bush/mission-philosophy--history.

Murray, Ryan. "Bailey-Boushay House exploring option of homeless shelter for HIV-positive clients." Madison Park Times. August 1, 2017. Accessed August 03, 2017. http://madisonparktimes.com/Content/News/Homepage-Rotating-Articles/Article/Bailey-Boushay-House-exploring-option-of-homeless-shelter-for-HIV-positive-clients/26/363/30908.

"Neighborhood Matching Fund Small and Simple Grant Project Records, 1990–2006." Archives West. Accessed July 08, 2017. http://archiveswest.orbiscascade.org/ark:/80444/xv12100.

O'Connor, Allison Marie. "Hamilton, John Henry 'Doc' (1891–1942)." BlackPast.org. Accessed February 20, 2017. http://www.blackpast.org/aah/hamilton-john-henry-doc-1891-1942.

O'Connor, Karen. "Community Invited to Celebrate the Gift of Julia Lee's Park." Seattle Parks and Recreation. October 20, 2016. Accessed July 08, 2017. http://parkways.seattle.gov/2016/10/20/community-invited-to-celebrate-the-gift-of-julia-lees-park/.

"Open Space: Central Seattle, East of I-5." *Seattle Green*, Summer 1998.

Ott, Jennifer. "Seattle City Council Approves Agreement Between Board of Park Commissioners and University of Washington Establishing Washington Park Arboretum on December 24, 1934." HistoryLink.org. January 26, 2013. Accessed August 03, 2017. http://www.historylink.org/File/10242.

"Our Staff/Mission Statement." MLK F.A.M.E. Community Center. Accessed February 20, 2017. http://www.mlkfame.com/our-staffmission-statement.

Pailthorp, Bellamy. "Seattle Park Is Giant Storm Drain." KNKX.org. September 6, 2013. Accessed February 20, 2017. http://knkx.org/post/seattle-park-giant-storm-drain.

"Prentis I. Frazier Park." RecPlanet. Accessed July 08, 2017. http://recplanet.com/wa/seattle/prentis-i-frazier-park.

Rochester, Junius. "Seattle Neighborhoods: Madison Valley— Thumbnail History." HistoryLink.org. July 25, 2001. Accessed February 20, 2017. http://www.historylink.org/File/3471.

Roskin, Miriam. "Our Local Scene: Julia Lee's Park." *Valley View*, issue 77 (August and September 1999).

Roskin, Miriam. "William Grose Remembered at William Grose Park." *Valley View*, issue 81 (January 2000).

"Seattle Public Schools, 1862–2000: Martin Luther King Elementary School." HistoryLink.org. September 8, 2013. Accessed February 20, 2017. http://www.historylink.org/File/10537.

Seattle Public Utilities. "Madison Valley Stormwater Project Update: Briefing to CDWAC." Presented by Celia S. Kennedy, November 14, 2012. Accessed February 20, 2017. http://www.seattle.gov/util/cs/groups/public/@spu/@diroff/d ocuments/webcontent/01_024642.pdf.

"Seattle Schools Wants Another Martin Luther King Elementary." MyNorthwest. March 28, 2011. Accessed July 08, 2017. http://mynorthwest.com/7458/seattle-schools-wants-another-martin-luther-king-elementary/.

Sheffer, Andy. "Arboretum Master Plan." Accessed August 3, 2017. http://www.seattle.gov/documents/departments/parksandrecr eation/projects/looptrail/arboretummasterplanlinks.pdf.

Sherrard, Jean. "Seattle Now & Then: Madison Trolley Accident." DorpatSherrardLomont. May 22, 2011. Accessed July 05, 2017. https://pauldorpat.com/2011/05/21/seattle-now-then-madison-trolley-accident/.

Smith, Craig. "Homer Harris, 1916–2007: Dermatologist a Sports Pioneer." *Seattle Times*, March 27, 2007. Accessed February 20, 2017. http://www.seattletimes.com/sports/homer-harris-1916-2007-dermatologist-a-sports-pioneer/.

"Summary for 1733 24th AVE / Parcel ID 9828200135 / Inv #." Department of Neighborhoods, Seattle Historical Sites. Accessed July 08, 2017. http://web6.seattle.gov/DPD/HistoricalSite/QueryResult.aspx?ID=394727438.

Sussman, J. "City Buys Land at 3001 E. Madison—Our Community's New Greenbelt." *Valley View,* April 1995.

Sussman, Jerry. "City Council Supports Harrison Ridge Greenbelt." *Harrison Denny Community Council Newsletter,* May 1992.

Sussman, Jerry. "Greenbelt Project Under Way." *Harrison Denny Community Council Newsletter,* March 1994.

Sussman, Jerry. "The Woods Get Another Chance." *Valley View,* December 1994.

Trethewey, Sarah. "Interview with Sarah Trethewey." Email interview by author, April 17, 2017.

Veka, Clay H. "Seattle's Street Railway System and the Urban Form: Lessons from the Madison Street Cable Car." University of Washington, URBDP 565: American Urban History, March 14, 2007. Accessed February 20, 2017. http://faculty.washington.edu/chalana/urbdp565/ClayVeka_Final.pdf.

"Washington Park Arboretum." University of Washington Botanic Gardens. Accessed February 20, 2017. http://depts.washington.edu/uwbg/gardens/wpa.shtml.

"Washington Park Arboretum Loop Trail." Seattle Parks and Recreation. May 09, 2017. Accessed July 08, 2017. http://www.seattle.gov/parks/about-us/current-projects/washington-park-arboretum-loop-trail.

About the Author

Isabelle Gray is a native Seattleite who currently lives in Madison Valley.

67689056R00051

Made in the USA
San Bernardino, CA
25 January 2018